JOSEPH

A LIVING, LOVING, AND OVERCOMING BIBLE STUDY

JOSEPH

...

WAITING ON GOD'S TIMING, LIVING IN GOD'S PLAN

MICHELLE MCKINNEY HAMMOND

with *Karen Ehman*

ZONDERVAN

Joseph Study Guide
Copyright © 2013 by Michelle McKinney Hammond

This title is also available as a Zondervan ebook. Visit www.zondervan.com/ebooks.

Requests for information should be addressed to:

Zondervan, *Grand Rapids, Michigan 49530*

ISBN 978-0-310-69636-0

The author is represented by the literary agency of Alive Communications, Inc., 7680 Goddard Street, Suite 200, Colorado Springs, Colorado 80920, www.alivecommunications.com.

Cover design: Faceout Studio
Cover photography: Shutterstock®
Interior design: Matthew Van Zomeren

Printed in the United States of America

13 14 15 16 17 18 19 /RRD/ 22 21 20 19 18 17 16 15 14 13 12 11 10 9 8 7 6 5 4 3 2 1

CONTENTS

HOW TO USE THIS GUIDE

GROUP SIZE

The *Joseph: Waiting on God's Timing, Living in God's Plan* video curriculum is designed to be experienced in a group setting such as a Bible study, Sunday school class, or any small group gathering. After viewing the video together, members will participate in a group discussion. Ideally, this group should be no larger than about fifteen people. If the total number of participants in your group is much larger than that, consider breaking into two or more groups.

MATERIALS NEEDED

Each participant should have her own study guide, which includes video outline notes, directions for activities, and discussion questions, as well as personal studies to deepen learning between sessions.

TIMING

The time notations—for example (18 minutes)—indicate the *actual* time of video segments and the *suggested* time for each activity or discussion.
   For example:

 INDIVIDUAL ACTIVITY: TAKING IT TO HEART 5 MINUTES

   Adhering to the suggested times will enable you to complete each session in one hour and fifteen minutes. If you have additional time, you may wish to allow more time for discussion and activities, thereby expanding your group's meeting time to an hour and a half.

FACILITATION

Each group should appoint a facilitator who is responsible for starting the video and for keeping track of time during discussions and activities. Facilitators may also read questions aloud and monitor discussions, prompting participants to respond and ensuring that everyone has the opportunity to participate.

BETWEEN-SESSIONS PERSONAL STUDY

Maximize the impact of the course with additional study between group sessions. Carving out about two hours total for personal study between meeting times will enable you to complete the between-session studies by the end of the six sessions. For each session, you may wish to complete the personal study all in one sitting or to spread it out over a few days (example: working on it for a half-hour a day on four different days that week). PLEASE NOTE: If you are unable to finish (or even start!) your between-sessions personal study, still attend the group study video session. We are all busy and life happens. You are still wanted and welcome at class, even if you don't have your "homework" done.

RELATIONSHIP
REVEALS YOUR
PURPOSE

Now Joseph had a dream, and he told it to his brothers.
Genesis 37:5a NKJV

VIDEO: RELATIONSHIP REVEALS YOUR PURPOSE
17 MINUTES

Play the video teaching segment for Session 1. As you watch, use the following outline to record any thoughts or concepts that stand out to you.

NOTES

Have you ever stopped to consider how your relationships affect your dreams?

Your three closest relationships mirror what your life looks like.

Your first important relationship in your life was the one with your parents.

We are not only born on purpose, but we are born with a purpose.

The most important conversation you can have about dreams is with your heavenly Father. He will plant the dream in your heart.

Proverbs 16:9 says, "In their hearts humans plan their course, but the LORD establishes their steps."

MICHELLE'S CLOSING QUESTIONS

- How would you describe your relationship with God?
- What parallels would you draw between your natural relationship with your earthly father and your spiritual relationship with your heavenly Father?
- In what ways has that earthly relationship had a positive or negative effect on your spiritual relationship?
- In what ways has your relationship with God affected your approach to life?

GROUP DISCUSSION 40 MINUTES

Take time to discuss what you just watched.

1. What part of the video teaching had the most impact on you?

2. Brainstorm as a group the many relationships a woman may have in her life. Fire them off one after another. Ready? Go!

3. Have you ever before considered the fact that a person's relationships can affect his or her dreams, either positively or negatively? Can you think of an example where this was true, either for you or someone you know?

4. Michelle stated that the three closest relationships in your life mirror what your life looks like. In what ways do you find this to be true?

5. Michelle also said that our first important relationship in life is that with our parents. A parent may be intentional and helpful, neglectful and even harmful, or totally absent. List possible effects on a person's life from each of these scenarios:

   • An intentional and helpful parent

   • A neglectful or harmful parent

   • An absent parent

6. Have one person read Ephesians 1:1 – 14 aloud to the group. Listen carefully as the passage is read for all the ways God thinks about us and all the things he has given us as his children. Then, as a group, list them and the corresponding verse below.

What God Thinks About/Has Given Me	Found in Verse

Which item from the list most stands out to you and why?

7. Just as Joseph's brothers tried to thwart his dream, other people may try to dash our dreams. Michelle said that remembering Deuteronomy 6:5 ("Love the LORD your God with all your heart and with all your soul and with all your strength") can help us keep our focus when that happens. Why do you think that's true?

8. Michelle talked about the fear of God—not a terrifying fear but a proper reverence and awe of him as our heavenly Father—and quoted Proverbs 19:23 in the Amplified Version:

   The reverent, worshipful fear of the Lord leads to life, and he who has it rests satisfied; he cannot be visited with [actual] evil.

   How does being reverent and worshipful lead to life and rest? And how, in turn, does it keep you from being visited with evil?

9. Take turns reading Proverbs 16:9 aloud in as many Bible versions as are present in the room. Share a time when you planned your way but didn't consult God about it. What happened?

   On the flip side, share a time when you allowed God to establish your steps. Why is it so much better to do life that way rather than making your own plans and hoping they are in line with God's?

10. Michelle stated that Joseph's close and loving "daddy's boy" relationship with his father was a divine setup for his destiny. Has there been a special relationship in your life that set you up for what God wanted to do in and through you? Explain.

INDIVIDUAL ACTIVITY: TAKING IT TO HEART
5 MINUTES

Complete this activity quietly on your own.

- Do you feel God has planted the seeds of a dream in your life—one that will glorify him? What is that dream? Write it down here in a nutshell.

- Next, take a mental inventory of the relationships in your life. Is there someone who you feel encourages you in that dream? How so?

- Is there someone who throws water on the fire of your dreams? How does he or she do this?

- Quietly pray, asking God to help you listen to his thoughts about you and not to the negative words of others. Bring your dream humbly before him alone to make sure it is in line with his will for you. Ask him to show you clearly. Then, if it is: GO FOR IT!

CLOSING PRAYER 2 MINUTES

Have one person from the group close in prayer. Then, get ready for some digging into the Word during your between-sessions personal study. Let the adventure and the dreams begin!

BETWEEN-SESSIONS
PERSONAL STUDY

DAY 1

1. Recall some big dreams you've had—even if they were silly—from childhood on. (Remember, Michelle wanted to be the chocolate version of Barbra Streisand!)

       Did any of these dreams ever come true? Which ones? For the ones that did not, what happened?

2. Look up the following verses and jot down what they have to do with dreams and plans and God's part in them:

Proverbs 15:22

Proverbs 19:21

Proverbs 20:18

Isaiah 8:9 – 11

James 4:13 – 17

3. Some Bible passages seem to speak of dreams as being frivolous and futile, an unproductive waste of time, and not in line with God's plan. Other passages mention dreams (goals, plans) with God as part of the picture. The question is: How can you have God-honoring, God-ordained dreams as opposed to meaningless ones? Ecclesiastes 5:2 – 4 says:

> *Do not be quick with your mouth, do not be hasty in your heart to utter anything before God. God is in heaven and you are on earth, so let your words be few. A dream comes when there are many cares, and many words mark the speech of a fool. When you make a vow to God, do not delay to fulfill it. He has no pleasure in fools; fulfill your vow.*

Using this passage as a springboard, list some principles about dreams, your words, and God's role. How do they work together?

Jeremiah 23:31 – 33 says:

> *"Yes," declares the LORD, "I am against the prophets who wag their own tongues and yet declare, 'The LORD declares.' Indeed, I am against those who prophesy false dreams," declares the LORD. "They tell them and lead my people astray with their reckless lies, yet I did not send or appoint them. They do not benefit these people in the least," declares the LORD.*

From this passage, what do you learn about dreams and their ability to be man-made or false? Is it possible to fabricate a dream or goal of your own and then "spin it" to be from God? Explain. Have you ever seen this happen?

DAY 2

1. In the Session 1 video, Michelle stated that God wants us to be made whole and holy. So, in a sense, God has a dream for us too! Read the following verses and then record what God desires for us — his beloved children!

   1 Peter 1:13 – 16

   1 Peter 2:9 – 10

Colossians 3:11 – 13

Philippians 1:9 – 10

2. A well-known and dearly loved passage is Jeremiah 29:11: "'For I know the plans I have for you,' declares the LORD, 'plans to prosper you and not to harm you, plans to give you hope and a future.'" But many of us stop reading right there without looking at the verses that follow. Read the entire passage slowly, letting the words sink in:

> *"For I know the plans I have for you," declares the LORD, "plans to prosper you and not to harm you, plans to give you hope and a future. Then you will call on me and come and pray to me, and I will listen to you. You will seek me and find me when you seek me with all your heart. I will be found by you," declares the LORD, "and will bring you back to the place from which I carried you into exile."*
>
> (Jeremiah 29:11 – 14a)

Based on this passage, what is *your* part in discovering God's plans? As a clue, look for the action words.

What is *God's* role? What does he promise to do? Again, look for specific action words.

3. When launching out to pursue a dream, what other factors should come into play as you seek to make certain that it is in line with God's will? Read the following verses and list principles you discover that will help you to keep your desires, goals, and dreams in line with God's plan:

Psalm 25:5

Proverbs 20:18

Proverbs 24:5–7

Psalm 119:149–151

DAY 3

1. Michelle made this statement in Session 1: "Our relationship with God determines how we conduct our lives. Will we strive or surrender?" On a scale of 1–10, with 1 being "I continually strive; I want to do it all on my own" and 10 being "I fully surrender to God

and his plan for me, letting him have control," how would you rate yourself in the following areas? Be honest. Only God will see this.

____ My job or lack of employment

____ My relationship with my husband or my dating life (if single)

____ My family members

____ My friendships

____ My home, car, and other possessions

____ My financial situation

____ My spiritual life, including being a part of my church

What do you learn about yourself as you review your ratings? If you see a pattern of striving rather than of surrender, why do you think that is so?

2. Look up Psalm 9:9 – 11 and meditate on it today, making it your prayer. (It is shown here in the Amplified Version.)

> *The Lord also will be a refuge and a high tower for the oppressed, a refuge and a stronghold in times of trouble (high cost, destitution, and desperation). And they who know Your name [who have experience and acquaintance with Your mercy] will lean on and confidently put their trust in You, for You, Lord, have not forsaken those who seek (inquire of and for) You [on the authority of God's Word and the right of their necessity]. Sing praises to the Lord, Who dwells in Zion! Declare among the peoples His doings!*

DAY 4

1. Joseph's relationship with his father was a divine setup for his destiny. He loved his father. His dad favored him. But this made his brothers jealous. Their jealousy caused many problems in Joseph's life, but it also brought him to the place God had already prepared for him before the foundation of the world.

   Michelle pointed out that in our lives—just as in Joseph's—so much has to be situated and orchestrated before a dream is birthed. How do you do during these times of waiting? Put an X on the continuum below to show where your attitude and heart usually is during these times in God's waiting room:

   _____

   I am patient and prayerful.   *I am impatient and fretful.*

   Are there times when it is easier for you to be patient and prayerful rather than to freak out? What contributes to this? Are there factors that help you to remain calm rather than anxious (for example, talking with trusted girlfriends, praying in a group, listening to your pastor, memorizing Scripture)?

2. Spend some time today memorizing these two short verses: Psalm 31:14–15a. Write them out on a note card and place it at your desk, your kitchen sink, or on the dashboard in your vehicle. Or make them the screen saver on your computer or smartphone. Anything

to get them off of the page and into your heart, mind, and soul! (A few different versions are provided here, so pick your favorite.)

> *But I trust in you, O LORD; I say, "You are my God." My times are in your hand. (ESV)*

> *But I trust in You, LORD; I say, "You are my God." The course of my life is in Your power. (HCSB)*

> *But I am trusting you, O Lord, saying, "You are my God!" My future is in your hands. (NLT)*

DAY 5

1. Read Genesis 37:1 – 17. List all this passage tells you about Joseph — his age, activities, relationships, words, job, etc. Don't overlook the tiniest detail. God included them in Scripture for a reason!

2. In just a sentence or two, sum up what you would say if someone
   asked you who the character of Joseph was in the Bible.

Now, get ready for the next session when Michelle teaches us about
Joseph, his dreams, and — more importantly — about yours! Let the
adventure continue!

YOUR DREAM IS GREATER THAN WHAT YOU THINK

Then he dreamed still another dream and told it to his brothers, and said, "Look, I have dreamed another dream. And this time, the sun, the moon, and the eleven stars bowed down to me."

Genesis 37:9 NKJV

REFLECTIONS FROM THE PREVIOUS SESSION
10 MINUTES

Take a minute to glance back at your answers from the Session 1 personal study. (Remember, if you didn't have time to do the between-sessions work, you are still welcome at the group meetings!) Was there a particular day—or even one specific question—that stood out to you? Something helpful or challenging? Share the day or question along with your thoughts and/or answers.

VIDEO: YOUR DREAM IS GREATER THAN WHAT YOU THINK 16 MINUTES

Play the video teaching segment for Session 2. As you watch, use the following outline to record any thoughts or concepts that stand out to you.

NOTES

Joseph had an amazing relationship with his father Israel. Israel was a man who had wrestled with God and found him to be faithful.

Joseph's dream was birthed from God's dealings and exciting adventures with his father.

How we view God will determine our expectations in life.

Joseph had dreams about his family bowing down to him.

The company you keep has a lot to do with how your dreams are formed and fashioned.

A dream takes time to come to life.

God likes to reshape our dreams into the dream *he* had in mind.

God is a God of process, and before any dream can come to pass, it has to die.

MICHELLE'S CLOSING QUESTIONS

- In what way has your personal background shaped your capacity to dream, and on what scale?
- What was a pivotal experience in your childhood that defined who you wanted to be or what you wanted to do when you grew up?
- In what ways have you felt limited because of your experiences?
- What dream has God given you? In light of your own desires, how have you interpreted that dream?
- How can God use your dream for God's kingdom agenda and for his glory?

GROUP DISCUSSION 35-40 MINUTES
Take time to discuss what you just watched.

1. What part of the video teaching had the most impact on you?

2. Joseph's father did not react to Joseph's dreams with jealousy as his brothers did, but instead he "kept the saying in mind." Has there ever been a time in your own life when family members reacted differently to something you accomplished or hoped to accomplish? Were some supportive and others jealous or even bent on ruining your dream? Tell the group about it. (But be careful in using specific names of family members.)

3. Michelle told of her mother's support of her dreams even if they seemed a bit far-fetched. Do you have a parent who supported, nurtured, and helped you reach your dreams? If so, what specifically did he or she do?

4. Parents aren't the only ones who pour into our lives and affect our actions and goals. As a group, list the various people in life who encourage or discourage our dreams. Starting with childhood and continuing to the present time, list those in authority, those in proximity, those to whom we are related, and those to whom we are not.

   Has someone in one of these categories had a major impact on your dreams personally? What did that person say or do to affect your dreams?

5. Michelle noted how our dreams may be only a small part of a bigger dream God has for us. This has been the case throughout church history: a man or woman had a dream simply to teach in the local church, but God opened a door that allowed the person to touch thousands of lives; a church desired only to feed the poor

in their local community, but became a global outreach center. Offer an example of God taking a little dream and turning it into a greater one.

6. When God seeks to bring about a dream, often he first has to wipe our slates clean. Why do you think this is necessary? What might be standing in the way of what God is trying to accomplish in us?

7. Have two people with different Bible translations each read aloud Isaiah 55:8. What do you discover from these different versions? Restate the essence of Isaiah 55:8 in your own words.

Has there ever been a time in your life when this concept of "God's thoughts not being our thoughts" played out? What happened?

8. Have someone read aloud John 12:24. What picture does the process of planting a grain of wheat paint when it comes to our dreams?

Have you ever seen — either in your own life or in the life of someone close to you — this process of death and resurrection of goals and dreams? Describe it.

9. In the New Testament account of the birth of Jesus, the wise men were told to return to their homeland via a different route, to go out a new way. When God tells us the same thing — to go out a different way than we came — why is that often difficult to do? What keeps us from switching directions or veering off the path we are so used to taking?

INDIVIDUAL ACTIVITY: TAKING IT TO HEART
5 MINUTES

Complete this activity quietly on your own.

• Is there a dream you have tucked away in your heart? Did you write it down during the Taking It to Heart individual activity last week? If so, refer to it. If not and you are ready to write one out, jot it briefly here.

- Now, are you open to asking God if there is anything in that dream (or in you) that needs to die first before his bigger (and better) dream for your life is revealed and comes to pass? Write a quick one-sentence prayer asking him to do just that.

Closing Prayer 2 MINUTES

Isn't it exciting to petition God for direction (or redirection!) in the unfolding of your little dream into the better dream he has for you? Have one person in your group close the session in prayer. Then, get ready for some personal study before your group meets again next time. Dream on!

BETWEEN-SESSIONS PERSONAL STUDY

DAY 1

1. During the Session 1 personal study, you read in Genesis 37:1–17 about Joseph's dreams as a young man of about seventeen. Take a moment to review that passage (or to read it for the first time if you didn't before).

   Now think back to when you were seventeen and the goals and dreams you had for life. What part would you say God played in them? Put an X on the continuum below to indicate your answer:

   ```
   ═══╪═══╪═══╪═══╪═══╪═══╪═══╪═══╪═══
   ```

   What God wanted for my   *I wanted God's perfect*
   future wasn't even on my radar.   *will for my future.*

   How about today? You still have goals and dreams, don't you? Now, place an X on this second continuum that shows where your heart's desire is today. Be honest!

   ```
   ═══╪═══╪═══╪═══╪═══╪═══╪═══╪═══╪═══
   ```

   What God wants for my   *I want God's perfect*
   future isn't even on my radar.   *will for my future.*

2. What happens when you do not invite God to be a part of your dreams? What does Proverbs 10:4 say about this?

3. Write a one- or two-sentence prayer asking God not just to join you in your dreams but to reveal his dream for you!

Day 2

1. Just as Joseph had to move forward to discover God's unique will and plan for his life, so do followers of Jesus today. Read Romans 12:2. If it is familiar, read it very slowly, as if you have never heard it before. Let each word soak deep into your heart and mind.

    What does this verse have to say about finding God's will for your life? What is step one?

    What do you feel is the "pattern of the world" (NIV) in relationship to pursuing a life dream? How do we "not conform" to this pattern?

2. What is step two when seeking God's will?

What are some practical ways to "renew your mind"?

3. Reread the verse. What is the result of doing steps one and two?

What do the words "test" and "approve" mean to you? (Depending on the version you are using, it may also say "discern.")

Day 3

1. In the video teaching, Michelle talked about the dismantling process God might take you through as you pursue a dream, and she stressed the importance of this step as a way to wipe the slate clean and allow God's bigger, better dream to be birthed in your life. What do you dread most about such slate-cleaning?

2. Below are some reasons God might temporarily dismantle our dreams in order to bring about his perfect and pleasing will. Look over the list for a moment.

- ❑ Pride
- ❑ An independent spirit
- ❑ An unwillingness to listen to or accept wise counsel
- ❑ Greed

- ❑ Arrogance
- ❑ Wrong motives
- ❑ Prayerlessness
- ❑ Bad timing
- ❑ Immaturity

Now checkmark any reason(s) why you think God either dismantled a dream of yours in the past or may be dismantling one today. Did you have a hunch this might have been an issue before now or did God just reveal it to you?

3. What do these verses say about this dismantling process and God's better plan being revealed?

Proverbs 11:2

Proverbs 14:3

Proverbs 16:8

Ecclesiastes 7:8

Day 4

1. Following God requires that we sometimes change directions, either because we didn't hear clearly from God in the first place or because he asks us to do an about-face. That very thing happened to the wise men at Jesus' birth. Read Matthew 2:1 – 12 and then answer the following questions:

    What was the desire of the wise men (Magi), according to verse 2?

    What was their reaction when they saw the Christ child?

    What do worship and bringing your gifts to Jesus have to do with discerning God's dream and plan for your life?

When their encounter with Jesus was over, they planned to go back just as they had come. What happened to change this?

2. How willing are you for God to send you off in a different direction than the one you had planned? How can you know that this change in direction is from God?

DAY 5

1. A seed is actually a plant in the embryonic stage covered with a shell called the seed coat. This seed coat helps to keep the inside from experiencing a damaging injury or from getting dried out. In order for the plant to germinate, the seed must actually "die" in order to release the new growth inside, develop into a mature plant, and produce fruit in keeping with its kind. Read John 12:23–28a and see what Jesus said about this very process.

   What did Jesus say about the kernel of wheat in verse 24?

How might the "dying" of a seed to produce a harvest be likened to our dreams dying in order to bring about the harvest God has for us?

What does verse 25 say about our priorities in this life? What might get in the way of reaching the dream God has for us?

In chasing our dreams, what is a very crucial perspective to keep in mind found in verse 28?

2. If you search your heart honestly, how intent are you that your dreams glorify God rather than elevate yourself? Are you willing to let your original dream die in order to allow God to bring about a greater harvest through the dream he is dreaming for you? Tell him so in the space provided.

Now, spend a few moments in prayer asking God to align your dreams with his. Then, prepare for the next session with Michelle as we learn how the trying times in life can allow us to either grow bitter or become better.

DON'T GROW BITTER, GROW BETTER

Good sense makes one slow to anger, and it is his glory to overlook an offense.

Proverbs 19:11 ESV

REFLECTIONS FROM THE PREVIOUS SESSION
10 MINUTES

Take a minute to glance back at your answers from the Session 2 personal study. (Remember, if you didn't have time to do the between-sessions work, you are still welcome at the group meetings!) Was there a particular day—or even one specific question—that stood out to you? Something helpful or challenging? Share the day or question along with your thoughts and/or answers.

VIDEO: DON'T GROW BITTER, GROW BETTER
16 MINUTES

Play the video teaching segment for Session 3. As you watch, use the following outline to record any thoughts or concepts that stand out to you.

NOTES

Genesis 37 says that Joseph's brothers hated him because of his dreams. Their jealously drove them to want to kill him.

Hope deferred makes the heart sick.

Offense is a distraction that the enemy uses to get us off point.

Matthew 18:7 – 9 speaks of causing others to sin. Cut off that which causes you to sin.

Even though we can forgive people, we may need to avoid the person who continually brings conflict back into our lives.

Offense reveals what we haven't surrendered.

Don't ask "why?" Ask "what?"

God is challenging us to get to the place where we don't grow bitter but instead we grow better.

The Judases in your life are necessary. Without the Judases, you will never go to the cross. Without the cross, you will never die. And without that death, you will never resurrect to the new life God has planned for you.

MICHELLE'S CLOSING QUESTIONS

- What offense has occurred in your life?
- In what ways did it affect your decisions?
- How did you handle the temptation to be bitter?
- How has offense distracted you from what God wants to accomplish in your life?
- How can offense be used to the good in your life?
- What do you need to surrender?

GROUP DISCUSSION 40-45 MINUTES

Take time to discuss what you just watched.

1. What part of the video teaching had the most impact on you?

2. Joseph's brothers called him a dreamer—and they weren't using that term as a compliment! Has there ever been a time in your life when you were called a name, labeled, or simply given "the look" by someone who was envious of you? How did it make you feel? What did you do or say to the person in response? Or did you choose to do and say nothing instead?

3. Discuss this statement: "The devil wants to kill your dreams."
   Think of a current dream (or if you can't, recall one from your
   past). Why would Satan desire to kill that dream? What would
   reaching that dream do to him and his plans?

4. Have different group members look up the following verses and
   read them aloud. What do the verses say about the devil and what
   he does—or longs to do—to Christians?

   Zechariah 3:1

   Mark 1:13

   Mark 4:15

   2 Corinthians 11:13–15

   1 Peter 5:8

5. Michelle said, "When people don't like you, they will hurt you. Or they at least won't do anything to help you." Without naming names or gossiping in any way, tell about a person in your life who fits this description. What was the situation and how did you handle it? Is there anything you wish you would have done in a different, more God-honoring way?

In what ways might we need to distance ourselves from someone who continually and intentionally seeks to offend us? What are some practical boundaries we can put in place to keep from being hurt and allowing old wounds to resurface?

6. Have two or three people read aloud Matthew 18:7–9 from different translations of the Bible. How would you sum up the advice in these verses in your own words? What drastic spiritually surgical methods might you need to take in order to get rid of offenses that lead to sin in your life?

7. Michelle said that offenses tend to reveal what we haven't fully surrendered to the Lord. When we cling to these "rights," they can become points of anger and bitterness in our lives. What relationship do *you* think exists between refusing to surrender and anger?

8. Sometimes anger rears its ugly head when we feel stuck in a situation, perhaps one (like Joseph) that we didn't even cause. Michelle challenged us to stop asking God, "*Why* is this happening to me?" and instead ask, "*What* do you want me to learn while this is happening to me?" How might learning to replace "why?" with "what?" help us to grow deeper in our walk with Christ? Can you offer an example of someone who did this?

9. What do you think about the concept of needing "Judases" in our lives to help get us to the cross so that we can die (to self) and be resurrected?

10. Review the list of closing questions at the end of the notes section. Which one most resonates with you and why?

INDIVIDUAL ACTIVITY: TAKING IT TO HEART
5 MINUTES

Complete this activity quietly on your own.

• Has there been someone who has offended you, perhaps even over and over again? What did the offense have to do with?

- What has been your usual way of handling this offense? Did anger play a part?

- Are you willing to allow God to use this situation to make you a better person instead of a bitter one? If so, write a sentence or two telling him that.

CLOSING PRAYER 2 MINUTES

Have one person from the group close the session in prayer, asking God to reveal rights needing to be surrendered or offenses needing to be forgiven. Then get ready for a week of study as you seek to become better and not let life's circumstances—or the people associated with them—make you bitter.

BETWEEN-SESSIONS
PERSONAL STUDY

DAY 1

1. Jealousy is a dangerous emotion that can cloud sound judgment and cause destructive behavior. Because of jealousy, people have lied, stolen, plotted, and even killed! When we are attempting to live out our dreams, it may cause others to be jealous of us and our successes and opportunities. (Or, God forbid, we may become jealous of the dreams of others.) What do the following verses say about the effects of jealousy?

   Proverbs 6:34–35

   Job 5:1–2

   Proverbs 14:30

   Proverbs 27:4

2. After reading these truths in God's Word, how would you sum up what jealousy does to the person who is jealous?

3. When others in your life — family members, friends, neighbors, coworkers, even church members — become jealous of you as you seek after God's plan for your life, it can put you in bondage. (You dwell on what they think of you or what they may be saying about you.) What is important for you to remember when interacting with people who are jealous that might help to set you free?

Day 2

1. Think back over your life for a moment and ask yourself, "When was a time that I felt greatly offended by something someone did to me, said to me, or said about me to someone else?" Briefly (two or three sentences max) write the facts of the situation, but *not* what you were thinking or feeling at the time.

2. Now chronicle your feelings through the entirety of the situation. For example, if your sister-in-law told another family member that she thought you were bossy and controlling about what food would be served at the annual family reunion, how did you feel when you first got the news? Were you angry? Defensive? Then, once you had a little time to process the situation, did your feelings change? Were you critical, wanting to point out times when your sister-in-law herself was a control freak? Then, did new feelings come into the mix, perhaps wanting to retaliate or say things in the hearing of others that would spin her in a bad light? List your feelings in the order they occurred.

3. God's Word holds the remedy for the many emotions we experience as women trying to navigate life. No more questions for today. It's time for YOU to dig into Scripture. Using an online tool such as *www.biblegateway.com* or an old-fashioned concordance in the back of your Bible, search keywords for verses that will speak to any of the feelings you mentioned in question 2. If you felt angry, search "anger," "angry," or even "temper." You can also search using words that are the opposite of what you felt. For example, if you felt anxious, search words such as "peace" and "calm" too. Record the verses and the gist of what they say below.

DAY 3

Revisit the situation you wrote about on Day 2 to answer the following questions:

1. When you felt offended, what did you do? For example, did you talk with others about it or did you go to the person who offended you and talk with him or her?

2. Having looked at the situation in depth yesterday, what did you discover from your Bible verse treasure hunt? Any guidance for how the situation might have been handled differently? Any comfort for you and your emotions that you discovered in God's Word?

3. Now—difficult question here, so get ready—if you are totally honest, was there any hint of truth to what the other person said about you? Were you blind to see or admit it at the time due to your anger?

4. If you could turn back the clock, how would you handle the situation differently, keeping in mind all you have learned over the last two days?

5. Okay, one last tough question: Is there anyone you need to contact to ask for forgiveness for your behavior in this situation? Spend a few minutes in prayer, asking God to reveal the answer to you. Then, if he does reveal someone of whom you need to ask forgiveness, ask him what that should look like: an email, a phone call, a handwritten note? Then, don't delay if the Holy Spirit is nudging you; do it today.

Day 4

1. We wrapped up yesterday talking about asking others to forgive us. Now let's flip the tables and talk about others whom you might need to forgive. It has been stated that being bitter toward someone is like swallowing poison yourself and then expecting the other person to die. How true! We think our bitterness is hurting that person when in reality it is only damaging ourselves.

In the Bible, the original Greek meaning of the word "bitter" has to do with a sharp, pungent quality that ruins pure water, making it no longer good or safe to drink. Metaphorically it is used in other places in the Bible to refer to the emotion of bitterness, which likewise taints what is good relationally, causing it to no longer be healthy or useful. Look up the following verses on this topic. Jot a quick thought or two after each passage listing all you learned about bitterness. Take note especially of its effects, what other sins it is listed alongside, the results of clinging to it, etc.

Acts 8:22–24

Ephesians 4:30–32

Hebrews 12:14–15

James 3:13–15

Now, time to craft a warning. Finish this sentence: *Being bitter is wrong in God's eyes and in reality only hurts me because* _____
_____.

If you sense that bitterness has been an issue in your life, perhaps it would be helpful for you to write out that sentence on a note card and either place it in your Bible or post it in a place where you will see it regularly. This will help to cement God's truth in your soul about this very dangerous and destructive emotion and resulting actions. Remember, you want your life's experiences to make you grow better, not bitter!

2. In the video teaching from this session, Michelle talked about the need for "Judases" in our lives. Having Judases (those who offend and even betray us) sends us to the cross. Only when we are crucified — and die to self — are we able to be resurrected to the glory and purposes of God.

   Learning to die to self is a painful process. It involves taking our eyes and our thoughts off ourselves and placing them on God. We learn not to throw ourselves a pity party, whining, "Why me?"

but instead ask, "What now?" As in, what is God trying to teach us though this situation?

Let's practice this question-switch habit today. Think of a current situation in your life about which you are tempted to think "Why me?" Then, replace that sentiment with a "What now?" prayer. An example has been done for you.

EXAMPLE

"Why me?" question:
Why do I have to be single still? It isn't fair my Prince Charming hasn't come yet. Almost all of my other friends are married. This stinks! Why me?

"What now?" prayer:
What are you trying to teach me, God, by the fact that I am not married? Am I searching for a romantic relationship with a man more than searching for your will in my life? Am I supposed to be learning to get my identity from you rather than from a ring on my left hand? What quality are you trying to grow in me to make me reflect you to others? Is it patience? Trust? What are you trying to teach me now?

Your "Why me?" question:

Your "What now?" prayer:

DAY 5

In preparation for Session 4, it's time to catch up with Joseph and find out what happened to him after he was sold into slavery. Read Genesis 37:18–36 and 39:1–23 and record the major "bullet point" developments of his story in the space below.

Whew! Lots of Scripture and soul searching these past few days! However, the hard work of allowing the painful parts of life to grow us into better, not bitter, women is God-glorifying and helps us move one step closer to his dream for us! You've done well. Now, get ready for our next session with Michelle when you'll learn about the process of refinement.

THE PROCESS OF REFINEMENT

See, I have refined you, though not as silver; I have tested you in the furnace of affliction.

Isaiah 48:10

REFLECTIONS FROM THE PREVIOUS SESSION
10 MINUTES

Take a minute to glance back at your answers from the Session 3 personal study. (Remember, if you didn't have time to do the between-sessions work, you are still welcome at the group meetings!) Was there a particular day—or even one specific question—that stood out to you? Something helpful or challenging? Share the day or question along with your thoughts and/or answers.

VIDEO: THE PROCESS OF REFINEMENT
18 MINUTES

Play the video teaching segment for Session 4. As you watch, use the following outline to record any thoughts or concepts that stand out to you.

NOTES

Joseph went from favored child to slave due to the jealousy of his brothers.

God usually uses us to make something happen for someone else that we would like to have happened for us first. We have to serve somebody!

God blesses us, breaks us, and then he gives to us ... over and over again.

The Lord was with Joseph even when he was a slave. No matter how awful the story looks, God is also with us.

No matter where we are, we should do our job joyfully as unto the Lord. Attitude matters.

Joseph was put in charge by the keeper of the prison. Favor and promotion come because of the presence of God.

Joseph was placed in the king's prison. God has a very deliberate plan of where he places you.

The only way that God can trust us to be good stewards is to do the inner work of preparing our character to receive blessings. This is called maturity.

God sees the end of the story even when we don't know where we are going.

Life will put us on hold until we line up with God's agenda.

MICHELLE'S CLOSING QUESTIONS

- What situations have proven to be uncomfortable for you?
- What has been your response to your circumstances?
- In what way can you see God at work even though you are struggling?
- In what way will he get the glory out of your situation?
- How can you see it all working to the good in the long run?

GROUP DISCUSSION 40-45 MINUTES

Take time to discuss what you just watched.

1. What part of the video teaching had the most impact on you?

2. Have one person read aloud Genesis 37:18–36 and another person all of Genesis 39. Listen carefully for what Joseph did and—more importantly—for what God did. Considering Joseph's story thus far—going from a favored son to a slave to a prisoner for a crime he didn't commit—how do you account for his amazing attitude and behavior through these circumstances? Did Joseph's attitude and behavior have to do with himself, God, or both? Cite Scripture references as your proof.

3. Briefly contrast Joseph's attitude and behavior with many "favored" people in modern culture (celebrities, politicians, etc.) who fall on hard times *of their own making*. Think of the kinds of things they say to condone what they've done or strings they might try to pull to get off easy.

4. It was during his time as a slave in Potiphar's house and an inmate in the king's prison that Joseph learned to serve. Look up the following verses about servants, taking turns reading them aloud and jotting down key words as you go. Then, as a group, compile a list of qualities that a godly servant must possess.

1 Samuel 22:14	Psalm 86:2
2 Chronicles 6:18–20	Psalm 103:21
Nehemiah 2:19–20	Psalm 119:23–24
Nehemiah 10:28–29	Psalm 119:125
Job 1:7–8	Proverbs 14:35
Psalm 19:13	Isaiah 65:14
Psalm 85:8	

5. The process of refinement isn't always pretty nor is it usually any fun! But God has our best interests at heart and he knows the final outcome. He will promote us in his own way and in his own time. What do Psalm 31:14–16 and 2 Peter 3:8–9 say about God's timing?

6. Recall a time in your own life when you struggled with God's timing. What was the situation? What were you feeling as the situation unfolded? In retrospect, how was God's timing far better than yours?

7. What did you think of Michelle's analogy of getting a "faith trophy case" to be able to look back at various trials God brought you through and thus gain strength for your current situation? Besides the Joseph story, give another scriptural example or two of God's care for his people amidst trial. What, if any patterns, do you notice?

8. Review the list of closing questions at the end of the notes section. Which one most resonates with you and why?

INDIVIDUAL ACTIVITY: TAKING IT TO HEART
5 MINUTES

Complete this activity quietly on your own.

- Think again about the concept of the faith trophy case: times of trial that God brought you through and used to increase your faith. If there were trophies in your case, what would be the inscription on one or two of them? (For example: cancer scare of 2007; death of my mother in 1998.)

- In just a word or phrase, write down the lesson you learned as you earned each trophy. It might be patience, trust, the power of prayer, grace, etc.

- Take a moment to thank God for awarding you these trophies and allowing you to view them as memorials to increase your faith in current situations.

CLOSING PRAYER 2 MINUTES

Have one person close in prayer, thanking God for the many trials the group has faced over the years and the growth in faith you have each seen as a result. Then, head back out to your homes and jobs to shine as servants of the Lord who trust not only in him but also in his perfect timing! Remember, he is seldom early but NEVER late. Be blessed!

BETWEEN-SESSIONS
PERSONAL STUDY

DAY 1

1. Let's start off this personal study by pondering serving. Has there ever been a time in your past when, due to your position in the family, workplace, or church, you performed in the role of a servant? Describe your role and tasks.

2. Now, how did you honestly feel about being placed in a servant role? Did you serve joyfully and eagerly or did you dread the menial work? On a scale of 1 – 10, with 10 being joyful and 1 being resentful, how would you rate your attitude? Why?

My rating: _____

My reason why:

3. Jesus was the greatest servant of all. Read Philippians 2:5–7 and record his attitude as he served.

4. How can you imitate Jesus' attitude as you serve today, whether at work, in the church, or in your family?

DAY 2

1. In this week's video teaching, Michelle stated that no matter where we are, we should do our job joyfully as unto the Lord. Attitude matters. When stuck in a dead-end job or performing a less-than-glamorous task, what does our natural ("in the flesh") attitude tend to be?

2. Now look up the following verses and read them slowly. (Reading them in a few different Bible translations may shed further light.) Based on the teaching of Scripture, what *should* our attitude be as we serve?

   Colossians 3:16–18

Colossians 3:23–24

Proverbs 18:12

Proverbs 22:4

Philippians 2:1–3

3. Based on your study today, sketch out a brief job description of a true servant of God. What qualities must he or she possess in order to please "the Boss"?

Day 3

1. There are no two ways about it: in life sometimes we have to wait. Wait for a promotion. Wait for answers to prayer. Wait for the truth to win out in a certain situation. Wait. Wait. Wait. When we are in God's waiting room, what is his goal for us? Look up James 1:2–4 for the answer.

2. Now, what action should we take if we feel we don't have the proper perspective in the waiting process? Read James 1:5–6 for the answer.

3. What is the warning in James 1:7–8 about our failure to believe and our tendency to doubt?

Day 4

1. From the outset of Joseph's life, he found favor both with his earthly father and his heavenly one. Even when Joseph was put in prison, God was with him. And Scripture adds that the Lord "showed him steadfast love" there. (Some versions say "kindness," "mercy," or "faithful love.") Why do you think it was important that the Lord not only showed Joseph he was favored but showered him with love at this dark time?

2. During times of trial and testing in your own life—when circumstances aren't rosy—how loved do you feel by God? Place an X on the continuum below to indicate your answer.

I feel abandoned and unloved.   *I feel wanted and loved.*

If you placed the X closer to the "abandoned and unloved" side, why do you think that is? What does our culture typically assume about God's love for us when he allows tough times in our lives?

3. Let's get God's perspective on this. Look up the following verses about why he sometimes allows us to navigate rough waters in life. Then write out a statement that accurately spells out God's purpose for tough times and whether he loves us any less during them.

Psalm 5:12   Psalm 66:20
Psalm 31:23   Psalm 86:13
Psalm 36:7–8   Psalm 103:11
Psalm 42:8   Psalm 146:8
Psalm 57:3   Proverbs 15:9

DAY 5

1. In her teaching, Michelle made both of these statements:

- *God sees the end of the story even when we don't know where we are going.*
- *Life will put us on hold until we line up with God's agenda.*

Pick one of these statements and write out your thoughts about it. Do you agree? How have you seen this truth play out in your own life or in the life of someone you know?

2. Based on what you are learning in this study about Joseph's story and God's timing in his life, has your perspective shifted at all when it comes to enduring hard times or times of waiting? How so?

Great job! You have completed Session 4. The next time we're together we'll hear Michelle share about the cost of righteousness. Until then, may you bask in the assurance of God's immense love. Even during the dark times, he is there and he delights in you. You are his beloved child!

THE COST OF RIGHTEOUSNESS

For though the righteous fall seven times, they rise again.

Proverbs 24:16a

Reflections from the Previous Session
10 MINUTES

Take a minute to glance back at your answers from the Session 4 personal study. (Remember, if you didn't have time to do the between-sessions work, you are still welcome at the group meetings!) Was there a particular day—or even one specific question—that stood out to you? Something helpful or challenging? Share the day or question along with your thoughts and/or answers.

Video: The Cost of Righteousness
17 MINUTES

Play the video teaching segment for Session 5. As you watch, use the following outline to record any thoughts or concepts that stand out to you.

Notes

Temptations will come. They are necessary to build our character.

We need a commitment to maintain righteousness at all costs.

Satan waits for an opportune time to tempt us. We must guard ourselves diligently.

THE COST OF RIGHTEOUSNESS

Joseph fled when Potiphar's wife tempted him to lie with her.

The enemy first befriends us and then he accuses us.

Sometimes it feels like righteousness doesn't pay off.

David blessed the Lord and didn't forget any of his benefits. He named them out loud.

We are in a war and we have enemies of our soul both seen and unseen.

MICHELLE'S CLOSING QUESTIONS

- What is the greatest barrier of your temptation?
- When is your greatest moment of weakness?
- How do you withstand temptation in your life?
- What safeguards have you put in place to walk in obedience to God?
- How much of your obedience is conditional to God giving you what you want?

GROUP DISCUSSION 40-45 MINUTES

Take time to discuss what you just watched.

1. What part of the video teaching had the most impact on you?

2. What used to be frowned upon by society is now winked at instead. While the culture in many ways used to support the Bible's commands, now many times it flies in the face of them. What sins today are thought of as no big deal by the world? Make a list.

3. How, when the culture is telling you that sin is not serious, can you maintain your resolve to pursue righteousness instead? What help can you glean from Joseph's actions? (Hint: Peek at the end of Genesis 39:9 for your answer.) How can recalling out loud that an action is a sin against God keep you from going forward and committing that sin?

4. When you hear the word "temptation," what other people from Scripture besides Joseph do you think of? And why do you associate them with that word? Did they successfully withstand temptation or did they cave into it instead?

5. Temptations are a normal part of walking with Christ. They come at us from all angles and at various times. Satan knows when we are most vulnerable and by what we are most tempted. Name some times and situations that might produce prime opportunities for Satan's attacks.

Why is it such a struggle to fight against those times when we are tempted to—as Michelle called it—fluff up our flesh? What is it about gratifying the desires of the flesh that is so enticing?

6. Take turns having group members read the following passages about temptation. After each, briefly note what you learned about God's attitude toward temptation.

1 Corinthians 10:13

Matthew 26:40–41

Galatians 6:1–3

1 Timothy 6:9

James 1:12 – 14

7. Michelle mentioned that sometimes it feels like righteousness doesn't pay off. We hang in there and make the right and godly choices, only to see others — who care nothing about the righteousness of God and following his ways — prosper instead. Can you think of a situation in your own life when that happened? What, if any, lessons did you learn about God and his timing because you had to walk through this storm?

8. What does the Bible instruct us to do when we are tempted? Read aloud the following passages — 1 Corinthians 6:17 – 19, 1 Corinthians 10:14, 1 Timothy 6:10 – 12, and 2 Timothy 2:22 — and then answer these related questions:

What is the common verb (action word) in these verses?

What picture does the word "flee" paint?

Contrast the word "flee" with the words and phrases below. How are these verbs and verb phrases NOT fleeing?

Stroll by	Consider
Walk away from	Talk to
Ponder	Flirt with
Reason with	Follow after
Stare at	

9. When we are diligent to honor God and fight against temptation, what does the Bible promise will happen to the devil? Have someone read James 4:7 aloud. YES! When we resist the devil, it is HE who has to flee! Brainstorm together some ways you have resisted the devil in the past. What have you done that has made it easier? (Note: Although it does get easier over time, it is NEVER a snap!)

10. Review the list of closing questions at the end of the notes section. Which one most resonates with you and why?

INDIVIDUAL ACTIVITY: TAKING IT TO HEART
5 MINUTES

Complete this activity quietly on your own.

• What temptation are you currently facing in your life? Write it here:

• How has today's session shed new light on what you need to do in order to stand up under this current temptation?

• Spend a minute asking God to help you to keep fighting the good fight, resisting the devil and fleeing from temptation in order to gain sweet victory in Jesus.

CLOSING PRAYER 2 MINUTES

Mix it up a little this time! If your group is able, stand up and link arms in a circle facing outward to symbolize your united front against the schemes and attacks of Satan. Take turns offering a quick "popcorn prayer" to God, asking that he would keep the devil from succeeding in tempting the members of your group to sin this coming week. End with a unified and hearty AMEN!

BETWEEN-SESSIONS PERSONAL STUDY

DAY 1

1. Joseph's temptation while serving Potiphar was sexual in nature, but of course not all temptation falls into that category. When in your life have you faced the strongest temptation? Describe what happened and what you were thinking and feeling at the time.

2. How did you react to the temptation you just described? Did you cave in to it? Simply flirt with it? Fully flee from it? Explain.

3. Now, as you think back on your walk with Jesus at that point in time, how would you rate your spiritual life on a scale of 1 to 10, with 10 being "closely following the Lord" and 1 being "barely walking with Jesus"? (Note: If you were not a Christian then, record a 0.)

My rating then: _____

Now, how would you rate your spiritual life on the same scale today?

My rating now: _____

If that rating has changed, either for the better or the worse, to what do you attribute this?

If it has stayed the same, why do you think that it so?

This week we are going to work on a Bible memory verse to help combat temptation. It is quoted here from the *Holman Christian Standard Bible*, but feel free to memorize it in a version you prefer. Each day of this personal study you'll be given time to practice learning and internalizing the verse.

James 4:7 *Therefore, submit to God. But resist the Devil, and he will flee from you.*

Day 2

1. Joseph's experience in Potiphar's house perfectly illustrates a truth Michelle shared on the video: *First the enemy befriends us. Then he accuses us.* Has this progression ever played out in your life or in the life of someone you know? If so, what happened?

2. What light does 2 Corinthians 11:13–15 shed on this idea? Read the passage and then fill in the blanks below.

Satan _____ *as an* _____ *of* _____. *(v. 14)*

Think about the word "masquerade." To masquerade as someone or something means to pretend to be that person or thing, particularly in order to deceive other people. What is it that Satan is pretending to be?

What does the term "angel of light" mean? First, what does an angel do? Read Matthew 4:11; Mark 1:13; and Psalm 91:11–12 for your answer.

What does light do? Think of it in its most basic form. What does light allow us to do?

To summarize, Satan pretends to be a helper who sheds light in our lives, causing us to see what we need to see. In reality, he is a deceiver who has NO desire to help us or point us in the way to go, but only cares about our destruction. That's why we need to fight back! Look over our memory verse, James 4:7, again. Say it aloud five times.

> *Therefore, submit to God. But resist the Devil, and he will flee from you.*

Now, without looking above at the verse, fill in the blanks below:

Therefore, _____ to God. But _____ the Devil, and he will _____ _____ _____.

DAY 3

1. Read the account of Jesus and Satan in the wilderness found in Matthew 4:1–11 and Luke 4:1–13. How many times did Satan tempt Jesus? (Note: Each temptation contained a phrase that started "If you …")

What did the first temptation have to do with?

How about the second temptation?

How about the final temptation?

2. These three categories of temptation are still the ones that Satan uses against believers today. He may tempt us physically, as he did with Jesus and food. He may tempt us with power and performance, as he did when he told Jesus to jump off the high point of the temple. He may even tempt us with possessions, as he did when he offered Jesus all of Earth's kingdoms. Of these three categories, where do you experience the greatest tug of temptation and why?

Did you notice how each time Jesus was tempted by the Evil One, he countered with God's Word? It's time for us to do the same. Again, start by repeating our memory verse, James 4:7, five times:

Therefore, submit to God. But resist the Devil, and he will flee from you.

Now, cover up the full verse above and try to fill in the blanks below:

James __:__ *Therefore,* _____ ___ _____. *But*_____ ____ _____, *and he will* _____ _____ ____.

DAY 4

1. Today let's dissect Psalm 27, which Michelle referred to in this session's video teaching. First, read the psalm slowly (and aloud if possible). Let each word and phrase sink into your heart and massage your soul.

   Which verses especially leapt off the page at you? List their numbers here:

2. Now, go back and choose two or three of those verses. In the spaces provided below, complete the exercise keeping these loved verses in mind:

   I loved verse _____.

   This verse tells me _____

   _____.

   It is important for me to remember this truth because _____

   _____.

   When I feel the devil attacking me in the future, based on this verse I will say to him _____

   _____.

   I loved verse _____.

   This verse tells me _____

   _____.

   It is important for me to remember this truth because _____

   _____.

When I feel the devil attacking me in the future, based on this verse I will say to him _____
_____.

I loved verse _____.

This verse tells me _____
_____.

It is important for me to remember this truth because _____
_____.

When I feel the devil attacking me in the future, based on this verse I will say to him _____
_____.

Now, let's see how you are coming along with the memory verse. (Note: It's okay if you need to look back at Day 3 for a little refresher before attempting to complete this exercise!)

James __:__ *Therefore, _____ ____ _____. But _____ ____ _____ , and he will _____ _____ ____.*

DAY 5

1. To wrap up our study on temptation, let's take our cue from Joseph. Genesis 39:9 tells us that, when faced with the alluring temptation of Potiphar's wife, Joseph responded by declaring this:

   How then could I do such a wicked thing and sin against God?

   Joseph didn't lessen the effects of sin in his mind. He didn't ignore sin, reckoning that it wouldn't be a bad thing *just this once.* He didn't assume he could go ahead and commit the sin and then afterward ask God's forgiveness. (After all, God IS a forgiving God, right?) Think of a temptation in your life that has turned into sin at least once. Did you ever use any of the above rationalizations when tempted to sin? If so, which one? Explain the situation.

2. Time for a do-over. Let's learn to say what Joseph said when tempted to sin: "How then could I do such a wicked thing and sin against God?" Write it out in your own handwriting here:

Now, the next time you are faced with a temptation, what will you say? Write it out again:

When you feel Satan trying to trip you up in an area where he has seen you fall before, what are you going to say? Say it aloud.

Now, for good measure, recite our memory verse for the week.

James __:__ *Therefore, _____ ___ _____. But _____ ____ _____ , and he will _____ _____ ___.*

Woohoo! Satan is on the run now! May God keep your focus riveted on him and your eyes and ears keen as you seek to recognize the schemes of the devil. Soon your group will be back together for the final session with Michelle: "The Key to Promotion."

THE KEY TO PROMOTION

Then Pharaoh said to Joseph, "Since God has made all this known to you, there is no one so discerning and wise as you. You shall be in charge of my palace, and all my people are to submit to your orders. Only with respect to the throne will I be greater than you."

Genesis 41:39–40

REFLECTIONS FROM THE PREVIOUS SESSION
10 MINUTES

Take a minute to glance back at your answers from the Session 5 personal study. (Remember, if you didn't have time to do the between-sessions work, you are still welcome at the group meetings!) Was there a particular day—or even one specific question—that stood out to you? Something helpful or challenging? Share the day or question along with your thoughts and/or answers.

VIDEO: THE KEY TO PROMOTION 17 MINUTES

Play the video teaching segment for Session 6. As you watch, use the following outline to record any thoughts or concepts that stand out to you.

NOTES

From the beginning to the end of a dream, it can take a lot of time.

The same thing that gets us into trouble is usually the key to our blessing.

Repeat cycles in our lives reveal the key to our blessing.

In prison, Joseph interprets the dreams of the cupbearer and the bread maker.

God loves for us to say, "I give up!" It is then that we come to the end of ourselves.

In the life of every person who knows Christ there is a Genesis chapter 41 where God flips the story in our favor.

The matter is not *if* we will wait, but *how* we will wait.

What are we doing, thinking, and saying while we wait?

God says, "When life hands you trials, let's make fruit!"

The desires and dreams that we birth in our hearts are for a greater purpose than just ourselves.

MICHELLE'S CLOSING QUESTIONS

- How does God turn past trials into good?
- What type of reference does it give you for your present situation?
- What do you need to adjust in your attitude as you wait on God?
- What type of support system do you need as you wait on God?
- What commitment do you need to make to yourself and God as you wait on his promises?

GROUP DISCUSSION 40-45 MINUTES
Take time to discuss what you just watched.

1. What part of the video teaching had the most impact on you?

2. Michelle stated that the same thing that tends to get us into trouble is also the thing that is the key to our blessing. For her it was talking. Can you think of an example from your life or someone close to you that illustrates this concept? For example, do you know someone who got into trouble by daydreaming in school but now is a successful fiction writer?

3. On an even larger and more crucial scale, do you know of someone who has turned a past tragedy or addiction into a ministry? How about someone who lost a loved one to a disease and now raises awareness and money for research? Or a person who once dealt with

substance abuse and now helps others escape its destructive cycle? This has been referred to as "turning your mess into your message." Give an example or two.

4. Michelle believes God loves to hear his children say, "I give up!" Why? What is it about coming to the place where we feel we've tried everything and are ready to quit that places us in the exact position where God can best work? Has this ever happened to you? Tell the group about it.

5. Have one person read aloud Genesis 40:1 – 22 and another read Genesis 41:1 – 16. Then answer the following questions:

What did Joseph become known for in prison?

Did Joseph use this skill to brag or draw attention to himself? Give a verse to back up your answer.

In Genesis 40:15 Joseph gave a timeline of what had been taking place in his life. Sum up what he said.

Summarize what happened two years later when Pharaoh entered the scene in chapter 41.

When Pharaoh discovered that Joseph had a knack for explaining dreams to people, did Joseph take personal credit? What did he tell Pharaoh? What do his outward words reveal about his inward character?

6. Michelle gave a twist on the popular saying, "When life gives you lemons, make lemonade!" when she said, "When life hands you trials, let's make fruit!" Can you think of others in Scripture, besides Joseph, who did this?

7. Have a few people read 2 Corinthians 1:3–5 in different Bible versions. What does this passage teach us about why God allows trials in our lives?

Is there a trial that you have endured? How might God use the pain of that trial and the comfort he gave you as you trudged through it to help others?

8. Review the list of closing questions at the end of the notes section. Which one most resonates with you and why?

9. As we approach the end of this study, if you could narrow down the teaching to just one simple lesson about life and our goals and dreams, what would it be? How has your perspective on the dream God has for your life changed since we began this journey together? How has your willingness to trust his timing also changed?

CLOSING PRAYER 5 MINUTES

Have each member share one prayer request based on the lessons learned in this study. Be sure to write down these requests so that you may continue to pray for each other after the study is over. You may even choose to assign each request so that everyone leaves with one person's request to commit to pray for.

Close with group prayer, where those who feel led say a sentence prayer thanking God for a truth he has revealed in this study. Before beginning, assign one person to end the prayer time.

Now, as you are dismissed, recite the memory verse aloud together:

> **James 4:7** *Therefore, submit to God. But resist the Devil, and he will flee from you.*

Congratulations! You have completed *Joseph: Waiting on God's Timing, Living in God's Plan.*

FINAL REFLECTIONS ACTIVITY: TAKING IT TO HEART

Complete this activity on your own at home after Session 6.

• What one takeaway struck you most about this study of the life of Joseph?

• For your last activity, write a prayer to God, committing your dreams to him and also trusting him with the timing. Then stand back and watch him work!

And allow me to add my own prayer on your behalf:

Father God, thank you for the awesome example you gave us in Joseph and for the privilege of walking alongside him on the pages of Scripture these past few weeks. May we learn to pursue righteousness in the face of temptation. May we be armed with your Word to combat the devil and his schemes. May we look to you for our significance and your dream for our future. We are your servants. Bless this daughter of yours as she closes the pages of this book. May she never be the same after this encounter with you. It is in your Son Jesus' name we pray. Amen.

Share Your Thoughts

With the Author: Your comments will be forwarded to the author when you send them to *zauthor@zondervan.com*.

With Zondervan: Submit your review of this book by writing to *zreview@zondervan.com*.

Free Online Resources at
www.zondervan.com

Daily Bible Verses and Devotions: Enrich your life with daily Bible verses or devotions that help you start every morning focused on God. Visit www.zondervan.com/newsletters.

Free Email Publications: Sign up for newsletters on Christian living, academic resources, church ministry, fiction, children's resources, and more. Visit www.zondervan.com/newsletters.

Zondervan Bible Search: Find and compare Bible passages in a variety of translations at www.zondervanbiblesearch.com.

Other Benefits: Register to receive online benefits like coupons and special offers, or to participate in research.